LEGENDS OF WARFARE
AVIATION

P-51 Mustang, Vol. 1
North American's Mk. I, A, B, and C Models in World War II

DAVID DOYLE

SCHIFFER MILITARY

4880 Lower Valley Road   Atglen, PA 19310

Designed by Justin Watkinson
Type set in Impact/Minion Pro/Univers LT Std
Front cover photo courtesy of Rich Kolasa

ISBN: 978-0-7643-5674-2
Printed in China

Published by Schiffer Publishing, Ltd.
4880 Lower Valley Road
Atglen, PA 19310
Phone: (610) 593-1777; Fax: (610) 593-2002
E-mail: Info@schifferbooks.com
www.schifferbooks.com

Acknowledgments

As with all of my projects, this book would not have been possible without the generous help of many friends. Instrumental to the completion of this book were Tom Kailbourn, Rich Kolasa, Dana Bell, the late Roger Freeman, Scott Taylor, Brett Stolle, and the staff of the National Archives. Most importantly, I am blessed to have the help and support of my wonderful wife, Denise, for which I am eternally grateful.

Contents

Introduction

Even today, almost eighty years after its first flight, the North American P-51 Mustang remains once of the most famous and recognizable aircraft in the world. Nimble and fast, qualities that led the Mustang to be used even today in air races, the aircraft was forged in battle.

Through the Anglo-Polish military alliance of March 31, 1939, and the August 25 Agreement of Mutual Assistance between the United Kingdom and Poland, the German invasion of Poland on the first day of September 1939 brought England into the war by default. In response to the German invasion, on September 3, Britain declared war on Germany, as France did as well on the next day.

Soon fully engulfed in the war, the English demand for warplanes soon outstripped the Royal Air Force (RAF) inventory, but also the capacity of the British aircraft manufacturers. This led the country abroad, seeking additional aircraft as well as other war material.

In order to obtain these goods yet also abide by the laws of other nations (notably the US) pertaining to the sale of war goods, the United Kingdom (UK) established the British Purchasing Commission. The Purchasing Commission was to act as the agent to negotiate for and purchase war supplies from North America, with the materials to be paid for from Britain's gold reserves. Arthur Blaikie Purvis was the director-general of the commission, and Sir Henry Self was the air representative of the commission.

From the outset, the British were interested in the Allison V-1710 V-12-powered Curtiss P-40, which they felt was the most capable US fighter in production.

However, the P-40 was the US Army Air Corps' first-line pursuit aircraft, and Curtiss's Buffalo, New York, assembly line was already working at capacity to satisfy demand.

Knowing that the British Purchasing Commission would also be shopping for bombers, North American Aviation president James "Dutch" Kindelberger approached Henry Self, intent on selling the Commonwealth the company's new medium bomber—the B-25—just entering production. Self, already familiar with Kindelberger and North American as a result of the Commonwealth's purchasing of the firm's T-6 trainer aircraft, countered Kindelberger's proposal with one of his own: Would North American be willing to produce the P-40 under license from Curtiss?

While eager for more business, Kindelberger was not particularly interested in producing an aircraft of another company's design, and which he felt would not have a long production run.

He countered Henry Self's query with a new offer—North American would produce a new-design aircraft, utilizing the same engine but offering superior performance, and do so in the 120 days it would take to tool up for P-40 production.

Given the proven track record that North American had established with the British, the Purchasing Commission agreed to Kindelberger's offer, specifying that in addition to being powered by the Allison V-1710, the new aircraft be armed with four .303 machine guns and cost less than $40,000 each, and that the first production aircraft must be delivered by January 1941.

Although already outclassed by many aircraft, both German and British, when a desperate British Purchasing Commission turned to the US aircraft industry in 1939, the Curtiss P-40 was the only US fighter in production deemed close to being capable. The British tried to persuade North American Aviation to produce the type through a licensing arrangement with Curtiss. *National Museum of the United States Air Force*

Curtiss, meanwhile, had refined the P-40 design, creating the XP-46—in an effort to create a product equal to that of the Commonwealth and Germany. While the XP-46 showed only marginal improvement over the P-40, there was enough improvement that the British insisted that North American purchase the wind tunnel test data from Curtiss. *National Archives*

The design of the new aircraft was turned over to Edgar Schmued. The company assigned the new aircraft the model number NA-73X, and Schmued and his team of engineers and draftsmen worked long hours rapidly honing the design.

Much of this energy was expended designing the wing. After repeated wind tunnel tests, the team settled on an airfoil designed cooperatively by engineers from North American Aviation and the National Advisory Committee for Aeronautics (NACA), the forerunner of NASA. The wing, designated the NAA/NACA 45-100 airfoil, was notable for providing a smooth, streamlined (laminar) flow of air around the wing, with a minimal amount of drag-inducing turbulence.

The NA-73X was rolled out of North American's Inglewood plant on September 9, 1940. Although the aircraft was not quite complete—it rested on landing gear from a T-6 Texan (a.k.a. the Harvard), and Allison was yet to deliver the engine, it met the British requirement of having completed the new aircraft in under 120 days. This was achieved by the company investing 78,000 man-hours.

With the engine at last in place, on October 11, 1940, the NA-73X began a two-week test cycle. During this time the aircraft was subjected to engine, brake, and taxi tests in preparation for its maiden flight.

Finally, on October 26, 1940, North American's chief test pilot Vance Breese climbed into the cockpit, pointed the nose of the NA-73X down the runway of Mines Field (now known as LAX), and took the new fighter into the sky for the first time. The first flight was brief, only five minutes, and comprised a few circuits around the airfield, but it gave every indication that North American had a winner on its hands.

Less than a month later, on November 20, twelve minutes into the aircraft's ninth test flight, test pilot Paul Balfour was surprised when the mighty Allison came to a halt. Balfour swung the fighter, now a large glider, toward Mines Field in hopes of returning home. But the field was too far away and the fighter too low for a smooth landing at Mines; instead the aircraft landed in a field of another type—a freshly plowed one. The landing gear dug in, flipping the fighter on its back and tearing away the propeller. Fortunately, Balfour was uninjured and the NA-73X was repairable, although those repairs would ultimately take fifty-two days. Also fortunately, the cause of the problem was determined not to be related to the aircraft design, but rather simply a matter of running out of gasoline in the tank selected by the pilot.

In view of this, tooling for production of the aircraft proceeded on schedule. A bit over two weeks after the crash, on December 9, 1940, North American received a message from R. F. Payne with the Export Office of the British Purchasing Commission. Concerning the aircraft, he stated, "We are to inform you that the above mentioned aeroplanes have been given the official designation 'Mustang,' and this name shall be used in all correspondence."

North American countered the British request to license-produce the P-40 with an offer to design their own, superior aircraft, and committed to putting a prototype in the air in 120 days, the same amount of time it would take to tool to produce the P-40. The result of this was the NA-73X, shown here, the prototype of the Mustang. *Stan Piet collection*

Only a single NA-73X prototype was built, and it is seen here during a test flight. The first flight occurred on October 26, 1940, but this photo was taken later, as evidenced by the red, white, and blue stripes on the rudder; these were not present on the first flight. The NA-73X had a natural-aluminum finish, with only those rudder stripes and the black antiglare panel atop the cowling breaking the finish. *Stan Piet collection*

Strangely, given how the Mustang would evolve, from the outset the British Purchasing Commission demanded that the aircraft be powered by the Allison V-1710, the same engine that powered the bulk of the US Army Air Corps fighters of the day: the P-40, P-38, and P-39. *General Motors*

The carburetor scoop atop the NA-73X cowling had a pronounced setback relative to the propeller spinner. At the bottom of the fuselage was the air-intake scoop for the radiator; this would become a vulnerable area for the Mustang, particularly in the ground attack role, and especially a decade later in Korea. *National Archives*

CHAPTER 2
Mustang Mk. I

Such was the confidence in Kindelberger—and some would say that such was their desperation for warplanes—that the British Purchasing Commission placed their first order for the Mustang on May 29, 1940, well before the first flight of the NA-73X. The contract paperwork assigned the aircraft, designated Mustang Mark I, the RAF serial numbers of AG345 through AG664. The first of these, fittingly serial number AG345, lifted off from Mines Field on April 23, 1941, with North American Aviation test pilot Louis Wait at the controls. Also, a second order for more Mustang Is was received. North American designated these 300 aircraft as model NA-83.

The second aircraft, AG346, was dismantled and crated for overseas shipping, arriving at the Liverpool docks on October 24, 1941. The aircraft was taken to Speke Aerodrome, where it was assembled and subjected to flight testing.

Whereas the NA-73X, like most prototypes, was unarmed, the Mustang I (not surprisingly, given the model number of NA-83) was armed to go into combat. Beneath the engine were a pair of .50-caliber machine guns, synchronized to fire through the propeller arc, and in each wing was an additional .50-caliber machine gun and a pair of .303 machine guns, giving the Mustang a total of eight machine guns.

Further flight testing of the Mustang in England confirmed that the type, while fast and agile at lower altitudes, was not well suited for operation over 15,000 feet. Thus, Fighter Command rejected the Mustang, retaining the Spitfire instead. The Mustangs thus were assigned to the newly formed Army Cooperation Command (ACC), where they would be used in an air-to-ground role. Plans were put into place to equip eighteen ACC squadrons with the Mustang, although ultimately only sixteen were so equipped.

The two aircraft of the preceding chapter, the XP-51s, were delivered to the US Army; the aircraft were actually part of an initial 620-plane order by the British for Mustang Is. That order was followed in December 1940 by a contract for an additional 300 Mustang Is. This is the first aircraft produced on that second Mustang I order, Royal Air Force serial number AL958. These aircraft were painted in the RAF camouflage scheme of Dark Earth and Dark Green over Sky, but those test-flown were marked with US insignia due to laws in place at that time preventing warplanes with another nation's markings flying over the US. Library of Congress

Whereas North American assigned model number NA-73 for the first group of 620 Mustang Is, the aircraft produced on the second order of 300 were assigned model number NA-83; however, they differed only in that the engines of the aircraft in the second order were equipped with a broad fishtail exhaust. *Stan Piet collection*

The first production Mustangs were the Mustang Is, of which the British received 620 under two contracts. Two planes from the first contract were diverted to the US Army Air Corps, and the service also flew some Mustang Is in Air Corps markings before turning them over to the British. The Mustang I shown here is such a plane, and it is painted in RAF colors: Dark Green and Dark Earth over Sky. The dark-colored feature near the left wingtip is a clear cover for a gun camera. *National Museum of the United States Air Force*

The four 20 mm cannons in the wings of this Mustang mark it as a P-51. The swiveling intake scoop for the radiator is in the raised position, its normal configuration during flight. The scoop was lowered during movement on the ground, for better air circulation to the radiator. Under the right wing is an L-shaped pitot tube. *National Museum of the United States Air Force*

A P-51 is viewed from the right rear during a test flight over a suburban area. The white disk on the side of the turtleback contains the North American Aviation logo, although it is very faint.
National Museum of the United States Air Force

Flying above the hills of Southern California, a P-51 is viewed from above. The relative locations of the 20 mm cannons are evident, and from this perspective, an especially clear view is permitted of the air scoop for the carburetor, atop the cowling. The cannon barrels protrude from tubes permanently fastened to the leading edges of the wings. A single landing light is mounted behind a clear lens on the outboard side of the outer cannon on each wing. *National Museum of the United States Air Force*

A different P-51 is viewed from above during a flight. This Mustang exhibits signs of heavy use, including oil spatters and grime on the wings, on the nose, and around the cockpit. Some P-51s carried their tail number on the rear fuselage, in large-sized figures. Visible on this fuselage aft of the national insignia is the number "137324," which translates to serial number 41-37324.
National Museum of the United States Air Force

The Mustang IA, the third group of Mustangs supplied to the RAF, featured two Hispano Mk. II 20 mm cannons in each wing rather than machine guns and omitted the nose machine guns as well. The wing-mounted 20 mm barrels were enclosed in tapered fairings. This Mustang IA was assigned to an RAF tactical reconnaissance unit. *Stan Piet collection*

The sale of warplanes, even for cash (as was the case with the British Purchasing Commission), required the approval of the United States government. As a condition of the July 24, 1940, approval of the production and sale of the Mustang to the British, the US government required that the Commonwealth deliver, at no cost, two of the Mustangs to the Army Air Corps. These two aircraft were to be built in the production run with those going to Britain, with only slight modifications as needed to accommodate US equipment.

The two aircraft were scheduled for delivery in February and March 1941. However, that deadline came and went without the aircraft having been completed. Despite this, on July 7, 1941, the US government ordered 150 examples of the type. However, the contract number for that purchase—DA-AC-140—belies the real intent. The "DA" is indicative of Defense Aid—that is, aircraft destined from the outset for an Allied nation.

It was (and still is) customary for governments to buy the engines for military aircraft from the engine manufacturer and then supply the engines to the firms building the aircraft. This was the case with this contract—and it was the delivery of the British-procured engines that was delaying the production of the Mustangs that were to be diverted to the USAAF. Finally, the Army stepped in and furnished the engines to North American, and the first US Mustang, designated XP-51, took to the air on May 20, 1941. That aircraft, serial number 41-038, was followed by the second, 41-039, on December 16, 1941.

Even after the XP-51 was delivered to Wright Field, the aircraft did not immediately enter into a flight test regimen. In part this was due to other aircraft having a higher priority, and in part it was due to difficulties in modifying the aircraft on the basis of a preliminary inspection after delivery. Furthermore, at that time there was considerable opposition to the P-51 from the upper echelons of the Army Air Corps, who strongly favored continued development of the P-40.

Ultimately, the final official flight tests were conducted at Wright Field from October 8 to December 22, 1941. In March of the following year the first XP-51 underwent flight testing by NACA at Langley, Virginia, notably becoming the first aircraft with a low-drag airfoil tested by the agency. Those tests consumed twenty-four flight hours. The late-arriving second prototype was first inspected by the Air Corps Materials Division's Flying Branch at Wright Field, then was dispatched to the division's Armament Laboratory for firing tests.

Impressed with the initial flight test results of the NA-73X, the British ordered 620 production aircraft. The British, who designated their aircraft by name rather than numeric code, dubbed the new aircraft the Mustang I. As a condition of the procurement contract, Britain was required to provide, free of charge, two of the aircraft to the US Army Air Corps for testing. The transferred aircraft were RAF serial numbers AG348 and AG354. The US Army Air Corps redesignated the aircraft XP-51s and assigned USAAC serial numbers 41-038 and 41-039 to them. This is 41-038, formerly AG348 and painted in RAF camouflage and markings. As built, the first several Mustangs had the short air scoop on top of the nose, as here.
National Museum of the United States Air Force

The Army Air Corps stripped the British paint and markings from 41-038 and refinished the XP-51 in the then-standard USAAC scheme of natural aluminum with red, white, and blue rudder stripes, and wing markings. Also, since the preceding photo was taken, the carburetor air scoop had been lengthened. Visible on the chin are the fuselage-mounted .50-caliber machine guns. Whereas the NA-73X had a one-piece blown Plexiglas windscreen, the XP-51s had framed windscreens with four clear panels. This aircraft is preserved and displayed in the Experimental Aircraft Association Museum, in Oshkosh, Wisconsin. *National Museum of the United States Air Force*

The Curtiss Electric prop blades have been stenciled with drawing and serial numbers and high and low angles. Beneath the nose, blast tubes extend from the muzzles of the fuselage-mounted .50-caliber machine guns. The machine gun ports on the right wing have been covered.
American Aviation Historical Society

The first Mustang delivered to the US Army, serial number 41-038, is seen here. Long housed at the National Air and Space Museum storage facility, it was subsequently transferred to the Experimental Aircraft Association. It was restored in the mid-1970s and flew in the Oshkosh air shows until 1982. The XP-51 now is on display at the EAA Aviation Museum, Oshkosh, Wisconsin. *Author*

A view from the upper right rear reveals details of the XP-51's vertical tail and right horizontal stabilizer and elevator. Also visible are the shape and relative size of the carburetor air scoop on top of the cowling. Fuel filler caps on the wings are painted red. *Author*

The empennage of XP-51, serial number 41-038, is seen from the left. The design of the empennage remained virtually static until the introduction of the tall tail on the P-51H. *Author*

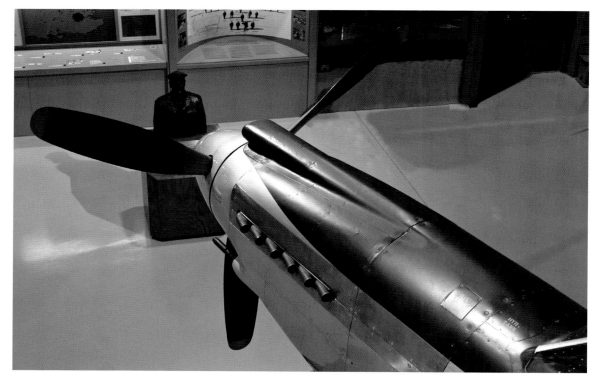

The rear of the carburetor air scoop on the XP-51 faded into the cowling about halfway between the propeller and the windscreen. On the antiglare panel to the front of the windscreen are access panels for the engine oil tank and the hydraulic tank. *Author*

Pilot and crew chief data are stenciled below the side panel of the canopy. Radio equipment is visible to the rear of the pilot's seat. To the left is a nomenclature and data stencil, giving the model, XP-51; the serial number, 41-38; crew weight, 200 pounds; and a notice to service this airplane with 100-octane fuel. *Author*

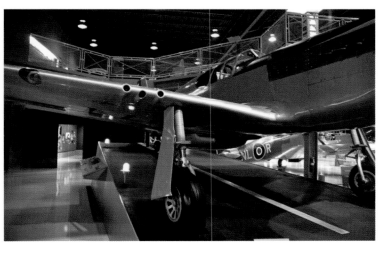

Like the British Mustang I, from which the Army's XP-51s were diverted, the XP-51s had three openings in each wing, for two .30-caliber machine guns and one .50-caliber machine gun. The muzzles of the outer and inner guns were just behind fairings on the leading edge of the nose, while the fairing for the center gun was below and behind the leading edge. *Author*

The air scoop for the radiator of the XP-51 is viewed from the front. The vertical joints between the fixed sides of the scoop and the swiveling bottom of the scoop are visible, as are the actuating rods inside the scoop. *Author*

Unlike the design of the chin-gun mounts on the North American A-36, the XP-51 (and Mustang I) had streamlined fairings where the .50-caliber machine guns exited from the cowling. Above the left machine gun barrel and forward of the exhausts is an access door for the coolant filler. *Author*

CHAPTER 4
F-6A

As previously mentioned, in July 1941 the US government placed an order for 150 of the aircraft to be supplied to the British. Because they were ordered by the US Army Air Corps, they were given a USAAC designation: P-51. However, the pressures of war and the need for reconnaissance were to change those plans. While ninety-three of the aircraft were transferred to the British, who designated the aircraft as Mustang Mk. IA, the rest of the aircraft on order were retained by the US and converted to F-6A reconnaissance aircraft. One of these conversions was performed by North American Aviation, while the remainder were depot modified. The aircraft were armed with four 20 mm wing-mounted cannons, with each gun having 125 rounds of ammunition. North American calculated their cost, before profit and without government-furnished equipment (notably engine, radio, and weapons), at $26,741 per aircraft. However, the final government investment in each aircraft was $58,698. Prior to receiving their F-6A designation, the type was briefly classified as P-51-2-NA.

The armament of the Mustang Mk. IA differed from that of the Mustang Mk. I in that it was armed with four 20 mm cannon, versus the mix of eight .50-caliber and .303-caliber machine guns used on the Mk. I.

From an order of 150 examples of North American Aviation model no. NA-91, the bulk went to the British, who designated them the Mustang IA, and the US Army accepted fifty-five, designating their planes P-51. The P-51, also designated the F-6A, was a tactical reconnaissance aircraft armed with two 20 mm cannon in each wing, and had two K-24 oblique cameras mounted behind the pilot's headrest, with a bulged window on each side of the fuselage to accommodate the cameras.
National Museum of the United States Air Force

Shown here is P-51 serial number 41-37320, which by the summer of 1943 was being used in performance tests at Wright Field, Ohio. Controversy remains over whether P-51s designated as F-6As had a third camera, mounted vertically behind the radiator exit flap. *National Archives*

The F-6A featured an oblique K-24 camera mounted behind the pilot's seat and aimed through a revised, bulged side window to the canopy's left rear. A second K-24 camera was installed to the front of the tailwheel, aiming downward. Wright Field technicians marked this photo with lines indicating the positions of the cameras. *National Museum of the United States Air Force*

The window for the cockpit-mounted K-24 oblique camera was blown, or bulged, to provide space for the camera. However, the lens was positioned to aim through a flat piece of glass secured to the bulged window with six screws. *National Museum of the United States Air Force*

This F-6A is finished in an experimental dazzle camouflage scheme developed by Capt. Paul Hexler. The scheme consisted of black and white patterns overall, except for the Olive Drab wing tops and a matte (probably black) antiglare panel. The US insignia was applied only to the top of the left wing.
American Aviation Historical Society

On April 16, 1942, the Army Air Corps issued contract AC-27396 for the production of 500 examples of a new type of the aircraft. Given North American model number NA-97, the new machines would not be fighters or even pursuit aircraft, as fighters were officially known; instead they would be attack aircraft.

Given the government designation of A-36A, the project provided the nation not only a needed dive bomber, but also a means to keep the Mustang production line operational at a time when the Air Material Command's position was that the aircraft had no future as a fighter for the US military and, in fact, was inferior to its contemporaries such as the P-40.

Despite being intended for an entirely different role, the A-36A externally differed little from the P-51. Most notable of these differences were the dive brakes set into the top and bottom wing surfaces. Also visible were the four wing-mounted .50-caliber machine guns, augmenting the pair of .50-caliber weapons mounted beneath the engine.

Beneath the wings were a pair of bomb racks, rated for up to 500-pound bombs, mounted just outboard of the landing gear.

While visually the aircraft differed little from the fighter variant, in reality 40,000 man-hours went into engineering a new wing to accommodate all these changes. The wing structure was changed to accommodate the hydraulically operated dive brakes, and key stress points were reinforced so as to tolerate the stress loads of dive bombing, as well as the bomb load itself.

Because the aircraft was intended to operate primarily at altitudes below 12,000 feet, the Allison V-1710-87 engine was selected, with its poor high-altitude performance not being a factor for the dive-bomber role.

Roll out of the first A-36A, serial number 42-83663, was in September 1942, with the aircraft's first flight the following month. By April 1943, the type was being used in the field, and in fact the first Mustang "ace," and the only pilot to achieve "ace" status while flying an Allison-powered Mustang, was Lt. Michael T. Russo, flying an A-36A.

Early in World War II, dive bombers were gaining notoriety as being particularly effective. Thus it is of little surprise that on April 16, 1942, the Army ordered a dive-bomber variant of the Mustang. The new aircraft, designated A-36A, came to be known as the Apache. The attack variant differed from the fighter in that dive brakes were installed on the top and bottom of each wing. A pylon under each wing was capable of carrying a 500-pound bomb or an auxiliary fuel tank.
National Museum of the United States Air Force

For strafing as well as air-to-air combat, the A-36As were armed with six .50-caliber machine guns: two in the chin and two in each wing. The wing gun ports are taped over, a common measure to keep the guns dirt-free until fired. On the leading edge of the left wing are two landing lights behind a clear cover, while on the front of the right wing is the pitot tube. *National Museum of the United States Air Force*

Just visible to the left front of the light-colored panel on the wing is the retracted left upper dive brake of this A-36A. The A-36As featured an enlarged carburetor air scoop to accommodate an air filter. *National Museum of the United States Air Force*

Little is known of this special pylon, mounted on the left wing of a North American A-36A, but it is reported to have been for a rocket, of type unknown. On the bottom front of the pylon is a fitting that may have been a mounting point for the rocket, and on the bottom rear of the pylon are two small sway braces. *National Archives*

Armorers are setting the fuses on 500-pound general-purpose bombs on the pylons of a North American A-36 with the 527th Fighter-Bomber Squadron, 86th Fighter-Bomber Group, at a base in Italy in 1944. To the far right is a Bomb Trailer M5 with another 500-pound bomb on it. The tires have a staggered, rectangular tread pattern. *National Museum of the United States Air Force*

An A-36A marked "33" on the cowling is armed with 4.5-inch M10 Rocket Launchers on the pylons. Note the diagonal brace running from the rear mounting strut of the launcher to the wing. The wing machine gun ports are taped shut, and tape has been wrapped around the muzzles of the chin machine guns. Several 4.5-inch M10 Rocket Launchers are on sawhorses in the left background. *National Archives*

North American A-36A, serial number 42-83707, with the tail number, 283707, marked on the fuselage, cruises below another A-36A during a training mission in the United States. This plane was written off after a landing accident at Hunter Army Airfield, Georgia, on January 8, 1943.

A-36A, USAAF serial number 42-83901, of the 27th Fighter-Bomber Group, was the mount of Maj. John "Jeep" Crowder in North Africa. The national insignia had yellow borders, and a yellow stripe was painted on each wing as recognition aids to distinguish the aircraft from a Messerschmitt Bf 109, whose silhouette it closely resembled. *Stan Piet collection*

Maj. Crowder poses next to his airplane, the dive brakes of which are in the deployed position. The number stenciled on the fuselage is the aircraft's USAAF serial number, 42-83901, sans the first digit. Above the serial number is a patch of gas-detecting paint, which would change colors if exposed to poisonous gases in the event of such an enemy attack. *Stan Piet collection*

Fully restored and bearing the nickname "Margie H," North American A-36A, serial number 42-83665, is on display at the National Museum of the US Air Force, Wright-Patterson Air Force Base, Ohio. Defining characteristics of the A-36 that are in view include the pitot tube on the right wing, twin .50-caliber chin machine guns, dive brakes, and the wide, clear lens on the leading edge of the left wing to cover two side-by-side landing lights. *National Museum of the United States Air Force*

From the side, the A-36A was similar in general appearance to the P-51A, save for the dive brakes and chin machine guns. Both planes had the widened air scoop for the carburetor, with an air filter in it, and both planes had the shallow, fixed cooling-air scoop on the belly. This was the third A-36A built. It was accepted on October 28, 1942, and was assigned to training duty at Eglin Field, Florida, during World War II. Under civil registration number N39502, the plane crashed during an aircraft race in September 1947. Later, it was rebuilt. *National Museum of the United States Air Force*

The left side of the forward fuselage of A-36A, serial number 42-83731, now nicknamed "Baby Carmen," is shown with a cowling panel removed to display the left .50-caliber chin machine gun. Below the gun's receiver is the 200-round ammunition magazine, to the rear of which is a sheet-metal box to collect spent casings and links. This box has an access door with a piano hinge on the bottom and a pinch-type lock at the top. *Rich Kolasa*

In a view of the right side of the cowling of A-36, serial number 42-83665, at the National Museum of the US Air Force, the six "fishtail" exhaust ports are in view. The barrels of the two .50-caliber machine guns that protruded through the chin had perforated cooling jackets over the barrels. On the cowling above the gun barrel is a square access panel secured with four screws. *Author*

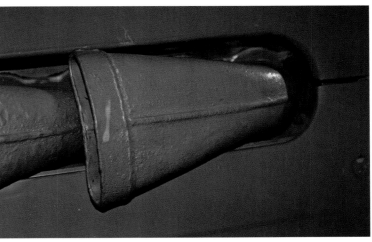

The forward fishtail exhaust port on the right side of the A-36 is viewed close-up. Note the weld beads in the form of an inclined T. The Mustang I fighter planes supplied to the British under Lend-Lease also had the two .50-caliber chin machine guns. *Author*

The right chin .50-caliber machine gun barrel is viewed from below. The muzzle of the machine gun protrudes slightly from the black, perforated cooling jacket. The chin machine guns were synchronized so as not to fire when the propeller blades were in front of them. *Author*

The air scoop for the downdraft carburetor is viewed frontally, atop the cowling of the A-36. In the foreground is the red propeller spinner. *Author*

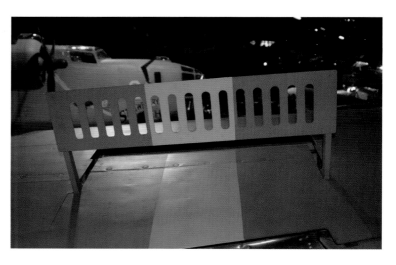

To lower the speed and improve controllability of the A-36 during dive-bombing attacks, a dive brake was installed on the top and on the bottom of both wings, four in total. The two dive brakes on the left wing are in the open position. These brakes were hydraulically operated, and each one had fifteen louvers cut into it. The left flap is also shown in the lowered position. *Author*

The right-top dive brake is viewed close-up from the rear. When not deployed for use, each dive brake rested in a shallow bay in the wing. *Author*

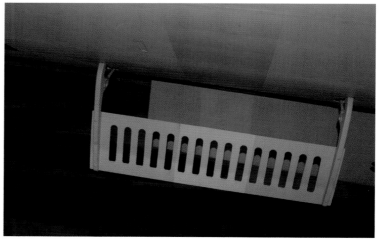

The right-top dive brake is observed from next to the fuselage. To the lower right is the lowered right flap. *Author*

The lower-right dive brake is in the open position, with the lowered right lap appearing behind it. The top dive brakes and the bottom ones did not have the same design; for example, as can be seen in this photo, the operating arms of the lower dive brakes were mounted on the outside of the louvered panels. *Author*

The A-36 could deliver two bombs up to 500 pounds in weight apiece, carried on under-wing pylons. The right pylon is shown here with a bomb installed. To the left is the bottom-right dive brake. *Author*

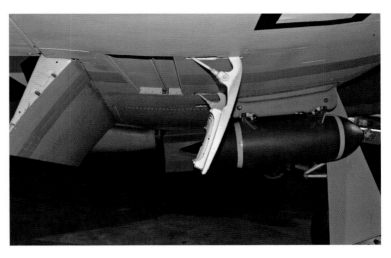

In another view of the underside of the right wing of the A-36, the lowered dive brake is at the center, and the lowered flap is to the left. The actuating rods for the dive brakes pass up into the wing through the same slots that the arms of the brakes are mounted in. *Author*

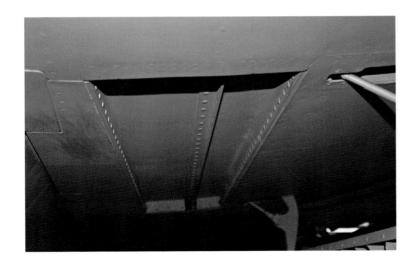

In a close-up view of the bottom-right dive brake well, an angle iron is riveted to the center of the bay for extra strength. *Author*

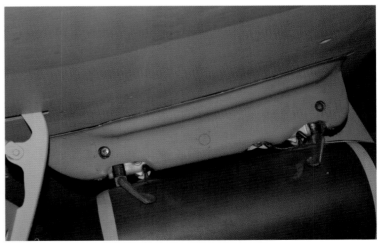

The right pylon is seen from its outboard side. The two objects on the bottom of the pylon that are in contact with the bomb are sway braces, to limit the lateral rocking of the bomb when the plane is executing maneuvers. Two lugs on the top of the bomb are engaged to shackles on the front and the rear of the pylon. *Author*

CHAPTER 6
P-51A

Finally, eleven months after the US Army's initial order for the new pursuit aircraft, none of which were delivered as such to the USAAC, on June 23, 1942, the subject was revisited. This time, contract AC-30479 called for 1,200 pursuit (as fighters were then termed) aircraft, albeit with some improvements. North American designated the improved new model the NA-99, while the military referred to it as the P-51A. Chief among the improvements was a new model of the Allison engine, the V-1710-81. The new engine, it was hoped, would provide better performance at high altitudes. The engine, like that of the A-36A, was equipped with a large filter in the air scoop, requiring the scoop to be enlarged over that of the original design.

Armament was four .50-caliber machine guns, mounted two per wing. Unlike the A-36A, no guns were mounted in the fuselage. Also housed in the wings were a total of 1,260 rounds of .50-caliber ammunition.

With a large contract in hand, and indications that more would come, North American set up assembly lines to produce twenty Mustangs per day. Indeed, this was a wise choice, because shortly thereafter a further 1,050 P-51As were placed on order. As it would happen, however, only 310 P-51A aircraft would be produced before a new, improved model was introduced.

The P-51A featured an Allison V-1710-81 engine equipped with a single-speed, single-stage supercharger, turning a Curtiss 10-foot, 9-inch propeller. This particular P-51A, USAAF serial number 43-6004, was the second P-51A built. The nose of the aircraft was adorned with artwork and the name "Slick Chick." Some P-51As, including this one, were equipped with a small, operable window panel on the side of the windscreen. *National Museum of the United States Air Force*

An Allison V-1710 engine installation in a P-51 is observed from the left side. Below the black-painted valve cover are the six left fishtail exhausts. To the upper rear of the engine is an air scoop for the carburetor, which is below the scoop. To the rear of the engine is the engine-oil tank, below which is part of the engine support. *National Archives*

The rear of the engine compartment of a P-51 with an Allison V-1710 engine is viewed from the left side. To the right is the oil tank, with the filler cap situated in a recess in the tank. At the upper center is the carburetor scoop, with the carburetor and the supercharger vent connection below it. The thickness and bolted construction of the engine mount may be seen. *National Archives*

The first P-51A, USAAF serial number 43-6003, was finished in an Olive Drab and Neutral Gray camouflage scheme. Here, the aircraft has been assigned to Ladd Army Airfield in Fairbanks, Alaska, for Arctic testing and equipped with retractable ski landing gear. The main landing-gear doors were modified accordingly. *National Museum of the United States Air Force*

The right gun bay of a P-51A is seen from alongside the cockpit in a January 1944 photo. The receivers of the two .50-caliber machine guns are in the foreground; above them are ammunition feed chutes, and the ammo magazines are in the bay in the background. The ammo magazines and the interior of the gun bay appear to be of unpainted metal. *National Archives*

The left main landing gear of a North American P-51A is depicted. Immediately above the top of the tire are two tow lugs. Above the lugs is the shiny-metal sliding part of the oleo strut, to the rear of which is the torque link. The landing-gear door is attached to the oleo strut with two links. *National Archives*

Specifications

Model	P-51A	P-51B-1-NA/C-5	P-51B-15-NA/C-10-NT
Production count	310	650	3,738

Dimensions/Capacities/Weights

Model	P-51A	P-51B/C-1	P-51B/C
Length (ft.)	32.25	32.25	32.25
Height (ft.)	12.2	13.67	13.67
Wing span (ft.)	37.04	37.04	37.04
Fuel capacity (gal.)	180	180	269
Fuel capacity (with drop tanks)	330	330	419
Empty weight (lbs.)	6,433	6,840	6,985
Normal takeoff weight (lbs.)	8,600	9,200	9,800
Max. gross weight (lbs.)	10,600	11,200	11,800

Power plant

Model	P-51A	P-51B-1-NA/C-5	P-51B-15-NA/C-10-NT
Manufacturer	Allison	Rolls-Royce/Packard	Rolls-Royce/Packard
Model #	V-1710-81	V-1650-3	V-1650-7
CID	1,710	1,649	1,649
Horsepower	1,200	1,380	1,490
War emergency power (hp)	1,360	1,620	1,720

Performance

Model	P-51A	P-51B-1-NA/C-5	P-51B-15-NA/C-10-NT
Maximum speed (mph)	390 @ 20,000 ft.	430 @ 25,000 ft.	439 @ 25,000 ft.
Cruise speed (mph)	305 @ 10,000 ft.	325 @ 10,000 ft.	325 @ 10,000 ft.
Climb to 20,000 ft.	9.1	7	6.9
Service ceiling (ft.)	31,350	41,500	41,900
Combat range (mi.; no d.t.)	750	755	1,180
speed/altitude (mph/ft.)	280 @ 20,000 ft.	290 @ 20,000 ft.	294 @ 20,000 ft.
Range w/ drop tanks (mi.)	1,375	1,450	1,900
speed/altitude (mph/ft.)	280 @ 20,000 ft.	290 @ 20,000 ft.	294 @ 20,000 ft.

Armament

Model	P-51A	P-51B-1-NA/C-5	P-51B-15-NA/C-10-NT
Machine guns	4 x .50 cal. Browning	4 x .50 cal. Browning	4 x .50 cal. Browning
rounds available	1,260	1,260	1,260
Bombs (lbs.)	2 x 500	2 x 1,000	2 x 1,000
			5 in. rockets

A mud-spattered, heavily weathered P-51A is being prepared for a combat mission at an unidentified airbase in India on August 7, 1944. A 1,000-pound bomb is mounted on each pylon; the fuses and fin assemblies have not been installed yet. Next to the bombs are 4.5-inch M10 Rocket Launchers, each of which has three launcher tubes for firing bazooka-type fin-stabilized 4.5-inch M8 Rockets.
National Museum of the United States Air Force

The majority of P-51As were dispatched to the China-Burma-India (CBI) theater, including this P-51A-5-NA, USAAF serial number 43-6151. The aircraft wears the diagonal white stripes on the fuselage and silver spinner tip markings of the 1st Air Commando Group. The national insignia includes white side bars, a style introduced in summer 1943. The P-51A has an RDF loop antenna on the razorback.
Stan Piet collection

Two 1st Air Commando Group P-51As serve as escorts to B-25 medium bombers during an attack over the Chin Hills of northwestern Burma. The Mustang in the foreground was nicknamed "Mrs. Virginia."
National Museum of the United States Air Force

The Planes of Fame Air Museum, Chino, California, maintains this very rare P-51A-10-NA in flying condition. This Mustang is serial number 43-6251 and is painted to replicate "Mrs. Virginia," a P-51A flown in World War II by Maj. Robert Pettit, 1st Air Commando Group. *Rich Kolasa*

The easiest way to tell a P-51A from the earlier P-51 was by the A model's lack of two 20 mm cannons in each wing; the A model had two fully enclosed .50-caliber machine guns inside each wing. Also, the P-51A looked similar to the A-36 but lacked the latter's chin machine guns and dive brakes. There were other differences between the P-51 and the P-51A, such as the A model's narrower carburetor air scoop atop the cowling, and the fixed cooling-air scoop on the belly, as contrasted with the P-51's swiveling air scoop. *Rich Kolasa*

Two firing ports are in the leading edge of each wing for the Browning .50-caliber machine guns. An L-shaped pitot tube is mounted under the right wing. The P-51A had provisions for a pylon under each wing, each with a capacity of one 500-pound bomb or a drop tank, to extend the range of the fighter.
Rich Kolasa

CHAPTER 7
P-51B

The marriage of the Mustang airframe with the Rolls-Royce-designed Merlin engine turned a good fighter into one whose reputation would grow to almost mythic proportions. The engine itself would become as legendary as the various aircraft it powered, having been installed in the Hawker Hurricane, Supermarine Spitfire, de Havilland Mosquito, and Avro Lancaster, in addition to the Mustang.

Even though the 1,649-cubic-inch Merlin had a smaller displacement than the 1,710-cubic-inch Allison, it produced 100 horsepower more at takeoff. Even more pronounced, however, was the difference in power output at altitude.

On both sides of the Atlantic, thought was given to mating the Merlin to the Mustang. One of the earliest considerations of this, if not the first, was the result of Ronnie Harker, Rolls-Royce's service liaison pilot, having an opportunity to fly a Mustang I on April 30, 1942. Harker had been invited by his friend Ian Campbell-Orde, wing commander of the Air Fighting Development Unit at Duxford, to fly Mustang AG422. The very next day he submitted a report to his superiors at Rolls-Royce advocating for the installation of a Merlin 61 in a Mustang airframe, opining that the combination would produce an aircraft 35 mph faster than the Spitfire.

However, when Rolls-Royce approached the Air Ministry, it met resistance, the ministry believing that the resources would be better spent on further Spitfire development.

Ultimately, E. W. Hives, Rolls-Royce general manager, was able to persuade that ministry to provide three Mustangs for conversions. As work on the project progressed, the Merlin 65 became the engine of choice, and the number of aircraft allocated to the project increased to five. Finally, almost six months after Harker's suggestion, on October 13, 1942, a Merlin-powered Mustang lifted into the air for the first time.

The Merlin had developed an impressive reputation even before the first Mustang took flight, and demand for the engine was exceeding Rolls Royce's capacity. Because the engine was felt to be critical to the British war effort, the Commonwealth and Rolls-Royce sought to license a manufacturer in North America to build the engine. Since in 1941 Rolls-Royce had licensed Ford to build the engine in England, it is not surprising that Ford was approached to build the engine in the US as well. While Ford Motor Company, Ltd., the English subsidiary of Ford, ultimately turned out over 30,000 examples from their plant in Trafford Park, Greater Manchester, it would not be the case in the US.

After Ford Motor Company, Ltd., received the drawings, did an extensive study, and agreed to produce the Merlin in the US, Henry Ford himself opted to decline the contract. Rolls-Royce then went across town to visit Packard, a luxury car manufacturer that was also busily building mammoth model 4M-2500 V-12 engines of their own design to power PT boats. Packard had no reluctance in building the Merlin, although the transition from Rolls-Royce's handmade manufacturing process to Packard's mass production techniques required considerable work on the part of engineers of both firms.

Thus, the Army Air Force was very familiar with the Merlin when Brig. Gen. Oliver Echols, chief of the USAAF Material Division, issue a contract on July 25, 1942, to equip two P-51As with Packard Merlin V-1650-3 engines. The new aircraft was briefly given the designation XP-78. The aircraft, given North American model number NA-101, carried serial numbers 41-37252 and 41-27421.

On November 30, 1942, about six weeks after the British first flew a Merlin-powered Mustang, North American test pilot Bob Chilton took off from Inglewood in the Mustang with a Packard Merlin engine ahead of him. While the conversions performed by engine maker Rolls-Royce in England were somewhat crude in appearance, the North American conversions, having consumed

40,000 engineering man-hours, presented a very finished appearance. In fact, the cowl appearance on all future Mustangs differed little from the two prototypes.

Test pilots on both sides of the Atlantic not only were impressed by the performance of the Merlin-powered Mustangs, they were excited by the capabilities and potential of the revised aircraft.

This excitement spread, not only through the airframe and engine manufacturers, but also the RAF and USAAF. Plans were already in place to produce the P-51B, as the type was redesignated after a brief flirtation with the XP-78 moniker, alongside the Allison-powered P-51A. However, after the initial flight testing, the decision was made to halt production of the P-51A after only 310 units, and to shift production exclusively to Merlin-powered aircraft, to which North American assigned the model number NA-102. The first flight of a production model P-51B took place on May 5, 1943.

In 1941, two P-51s were set aside to use as experimental test beds for the installation of powerful Packard Merlin engines (Rolls-Royce Merlins license-built in the United States). The modified aircraft were designated XP-51Bs and were equipped with four-bladed Hamilton Standard 24D50-65 cuffed propellers. In order to accommodate the new engine, the cowling was redesigned, with different panel lines than on the P-51 and with the carburetor air scoop moved to the bottom of the cowling as needed by the Merlin engine's updraft system. This, the first XP-51B, did not have guns installed.
National Museum of the United States Air Force

For the P-51B, the Allison V-1710-81 (F20R) engine was replaced by the much more powerful Packard V-1650 Merlin engine, a license-built version of the Rolls-Royce Merlin. The Packard V-1650 was a twelve-cylinder, Vee, liquid-cooled engine with a 1,649-cubic-inch displacement. Whereas the Allison engine had a single-stage supercharger, the Packard engine received a potent boost from a two-speed, two-stage, intercooled supercharger, which allowed the aircraft to operate at much-higher altitudes than Mustangs with Allison engines. The Packard V-1650 had a dry weight of 1,645 pounds.
National Museum of the United States Air Force

The same Packard V-1650 Merlin engine shown in the preceding photo is viewed from the right front on a wooden stand. In the foreground is the propeller shaft, issuing out of the propeller-drive and front-races case. Along the upper part of the side of the engine block are six exhaust ports, to which individual exhaust stacks will be attached. Atop the engine are coolant outlet pipes. *National Museum of the United States Air Force*

A Packard V-1650 Merlin engine is viewed from the left side. Temporary covers are bolted to the exhaust ports. The box-shaped object with X-type reinforcing on the side is the intercooler. Below the intercooler on the rear of the engine is the supercharger, at the bottom of which is the carburetor. Underneath the oil pan are dual fuel pumps and the oil pump. *National Museum of the United States Air Force*

Because the Packard Merlin was more powerful than the Allison V-1710, the Packard had a completely different engine mount. Note the cylindrical exhausts, as opposed to the fishtail exhausts of the Allison engine. Another Packard Merlin with propeller installed is visible behind clear plastic in the left background. *National Museum of the United States Air Force*

While the first XP-51B lacked weapons, the second XP-51B was armed with two 20 mm cannons in each wing. Just outboard of the 20 mm cannon is a landing light in the leading edge of the left wing. The insignia on the vertical tail of this aircraft is that of North American Aviation. *National Museum of the United States Air Force*

The second XP-51B is viewed from the front, providing a straight-on view of the Hamilton Standard cuffed propeller. The XP-51B attained a speed of 441 mph at 29,800 feet, which was over 100 mph more than Allison-powered P-51s at that altitude. *National Museum of the United States Air Force*

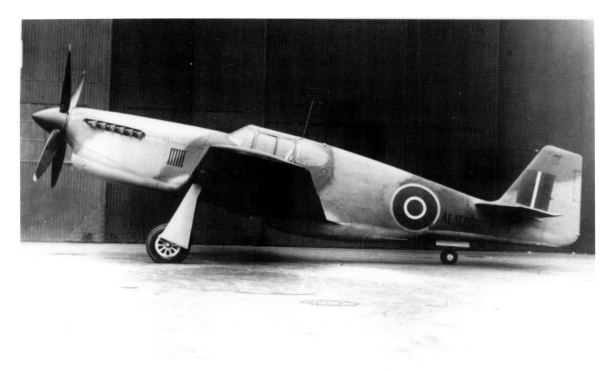

Rolls-Royce employed the RAF's Mustang I serial number AL 975/G in experiments with mounting a Rolls-Royce Merlin engine in place of the Allison engine. This involved fabricating a new cowling with a large intake for carburetor air on the chin. This plane was the prototype for the Mustang X; it was converted in July 1942 and first flew as a Mustang X on October 13, 1942. A total of five airframes were converted to Mustang Xs. *San Diego Air and Space Museum*

The British experimented with several different installations of Rolls-Royce Merlin engines in multiple Mustangs, all of them being designated Mustang X. The large carburetor air scoop and the extended dorsal fin that were characteristics of these conversions are plainly visible on this one, serial number AL963. *National Museum of the United States Air Force*

The Merlin-powered P-51B, with its two-speed, two-stage supercharger, was the first production version of the Mustang truly fit for high-altitude combat. Armament consisted of two .50-caliber machine guns mounted in each wing. One of these aircraft, North American P-51B-1-NA, USAAF serial number 43-12201, passes over the California coast on a test flight in 1943. *Stan Piet collection*

This P-51B, serial number 43-12408, was one of 400, with serial numbers 43-12093 to 43-12492, built in the P-51B-1-NA production block. Three additional blocks were built, raising total P-51B production to 1,900 aircraft. Faintly visible just outboard of the main landing-gear doors are pylons for a bomb or an auxiliary fuel tank. *Stan Piet collection*

The fuselage of the P-51B was considerably different from that of earlier Mustangs. Most of these changes were made in order to accommodate the Packard Merlin. The carburetor air scoop was enlarged and moved to the bottom of the cowling, and the cooling-air scoop on the bottom of the fuselage was made deeper. Not surprisingly, the lines of the panels of the cowling also had changed, and round exhaust stubs were used rather than the fishtail stubs of the late Allison-powered aircraft. Under the wings of this factory-fresh Olive Drab over Neutral Gray P-51B are metal 75-gallon auxiliary fuel tanks. These drop tanks substantially increased the range of the P-51s. Beginning with the P-51B-10-NA production block, an 85-gallon fuel tank would be installed behind the cockpit, increasing the range even more. *Stan Piet collection*

"Snoot's Sniper" was the nickname of P-51B-10-NA, serial number 42-106703, assigned to the 328th Fighter Squadron, 352nd Fighter Group, and photographed at RAF Mount Farm. The aircraft, which was flown by Lt. Francis W. Horne, was named to reflect the crew chief, SSgt. Art "Snoot" Snyder—who was a barber. It was supposed to be named "Snoot's Snipper"—but the artist made a mistake. The "barber pole" on the tail also reflects the intent. The "S" character of the PE-S code was painted on the vertical tail. Eight swastikas, denoting kills, are painted beneath the Malcolm hood–equipped cockpit. *Roger Freeman collection*

The small white cross on the fuselage of "Snoot's Sniper" indicated that the plane was equipped with a fuselage fuel tank, which radically affected the aircraft's center of gravity. Eight swastika kill markings are visible on the side of the cockpit, and a red-and-white border was painted around the dark-blue paint on the nose. *Stan Piet collection*

Armorers service a .50-caliber machine gun in the left wing of a P-51B at a base in England. Because of a tendency for ammunition trays to shift, causing kinks in the ammo belts, jams were a frequent problem for pilots of P-51Bs and P-51Cs. This aircraft was assigned to the 336th Fighter Squadron, part of the 4th Fighter Group, as indicated by the "VF" fuselage code. A small door covering an external power socket is visible just below the "V." *National Archives*

The P-51B carried 1,260 rounds of .50-caliber ammunition. Here, an armorer of the 9th Fighter Command at Boxted, England, lays the belts into the ammunition tray of a P-51B on January 20, 1944. In the background, two mechanics give attention to the rear of the Merlin engine. *National Archives*

Lt. Edward Ondris of the 358th Fighter Squadron, 355th Fighter Group, was the pilot of "Big Dog's Ellen Jean," P-51B-10-NA, serial number 43-7147, YF-M. The nickname honored Ondris's moniker, "Big Dog," and his wife, Ellen Jean. This Mustang suffered structural failure during a dogfight between Emmen and Emden, Germany, in early April 1944, in which Lt. Ondris was killed in action. *Roger Freeman collection*

P-51B-5-NA, serial number 43-6834, YF-G, nicknamed "the Great McGinty," served with the 358th Fighter Squadron, 355th Fighter Group, 8th Air Force. This Mustang crashed after being hit by flak while strafing a train near Vechta, Germany, on August 15, 1944. *Roger Freeman collection*

After evidently having its left wing shot up during a combat mission, a P-51B from the 368th Fighter Squadron, 359th Fighter Group, heads into a hangar for repairs. Two different P-51Bs from the 368th Fighter Squadron bore the fuselage code CV-M at different times: serial numbers 42-106474 and 42-106693. Both serial numbers are compatible with what is visible of the tail number: 21.
National Museum of the United States Air Force

"Man o' War," P-51B-5-NA, serial number 43-6431, WR-A, was one of several aircraft flown by Lt. Col. Claiborne Holmes Kinnard Jr., the majority of which he gave that name to. This Mustang was assigned to the 354th Fighter Squadron, 355th Fighter Group, 8th Air Force, based at RAF Steeple Morden, England, of which Kinnard was the commanding officer. The nickname was painted in white on the red paint to the front of the cockpit. This aircraft was in a midair collision near Steeple Morden, England, on July 16, 1944; the pilot at that time, Norman E. McDonald, survived but was later killed in action in October 1944.
Roger Freeman collection

"The Iowa Beaut" was a P-51B-15-NA, serial number 42-106950, of the 354th Fighter Squadron, 355th Fighter Group. Originally named "Man o' War" and flown by Lt. Col. Claiborne Kinnard, the aircraft was later assigned to Lt. Robert Hulderman, who renamed it "the Iowa Beaut" but retained Kinnard's victory markings. In this July 1944 photo, the aircraft is being flown by Lt. Lee Mendenhall. *National Archives*

The distinctive black-and-white stripes and spinner bands of the 20th Fighter Group's Mustangs are present on P-51B-5, serial number 43-6865, fuselage code KI-Q, of the 55th Fighter Squadron. The plane is marked "WW" for war weary after the tail number. Remnants of invasion stripes are on the belly. Sometime after this photo was taken, this plane was converted to a TP-51B dual-control, two-seat trainer aircraft, painted overall yellow and flown by the 479th Fighter Group. *Roger Freeman collection*

"Swede" was the nickname painted on the cowling of P-51B-15-NA, serial number 42-106886, coded 5Q-O, with the 504th Fighter Squadron, 339th Fighter Group, parked at RAF Mount Farm. The spinner and nose were red and white, while the rudder was painted green. *Roger Freeman collection*

Famed ace Dominic "Don" Gentile of the 4th Fighter Squadron, 336th Fighter Group, who scored half of his thirty kills while flying a P-51B Mustang, poses in the cockpit. This aircraft, P-51B-5-NA, serial number 43-6913, coded VF-T, named "Shangri-La," was destroyed on April 13, 1944, while Gentile was showboating for reporters at RAF Debden. His incensed commanding officer, the equally legendary Col. Don Blakeslee, grounded him on the spot and sent him back to the US for a War Bond tour.
Stan Piet collection

On D-day, June 6, 1944, P-51 Mustangs of the 361st Fighter Group are warming their engines preparatory to a combat mission, at RAF Bottisham. In the right foreground is "Bald Eagle III," P-51B-15-NA, serial number 42-106839, code B7-E, of the 374th Fighter Squadron. The bubbletop Mustang just beyond "Bald Eagle III" is "Vi," P-51D-5-NA, serial number 44-13391, and code E9-K, from the 376th Fighter Squadron. *Roger Freeman collection*

"Queen Jean," P-51B-15-NA, serial number 42-106875, and fuselage code E2-D, of the 375th Fighter Squadron, 361st Fighter Group, prepares for takeoff at RAF Bottisham. On the lower part of the cowling is painted an ace of spades, superimposed on a circle with red and white stripes. *Roger Freeman collection*

Capt. Harvey F. Mace of the 362nd Fighter Squadron, 357th Fighter Group, poses next to his P-51B, nicknamed "Sweet Helen" after his wife, at RAF Leiston, in Suffolk, England. "Sweet Helen" was P-51B-5-NA, serial number 43-6923, and fuselage code G4-O. After World War II, Mace (1921–2013) continued to fly, as a crop duster, an aerial photographer, and a participant in air races at Reno, Nevada. *Roger Freeman collection*

At the bottom center, a crew chief with the 355th Fighter Group is making adjustments to the engine of "Woody's Maytag," P-51B-5-NA, serial number 43-6520, WR-W, from the 354th Fighter Squadron. "Woody's Maytag" was shot down by flak near St.-Quentin, France, on June 4, 1944, with the loss of the pilot, Henry W. Davis. *Roger Freeman collection*

The same crew chief shown in the preceding photo is seen from farther back while working on the engine of "Woody's Maytag." Note the yellowish-green zinc chromate primer on the engine mount and on the oil tank on the front of the firewall, and on the reinforcing strip on the otherwise silver-colored interior of the inner main-gear door. The frame members of the fuselage, to which the cowling panels were fastened, are silver colored. *Roger Freeman collection*

In August 1944, Major Enoch B. Stephenson Jr. of the 503rd Fighter Squadron (FS), 339th Fighter Group, is about to enter the cockpit of his razorback P-51B, serial number 42-24803, equipped with a Malcolm hood. The "D7" squadron code for the 503rd FS is on the fuselage. A 500-pound is mounted on the pylon. *Roger Freeman collection*

Maj. Enoch B. Stephenson Jr. smiles for the camera in the cockpit of his Mustang. Born in 1918, he joined the Army Air Forces in July 1942 and was assigned to the 339th Fighter Group as a 2nd lieutenant in September 1943. During his stint with the squadron, he flew sixty-six combat missions in P-51 Mustangs and received several decorations, including the Distinguished Flying Cross. He retired as a brigadier general in the Tennessee Air National Guard after thirty-one years of service and died at age ninety-three on January 21, 2012. *Roger Freeman collection*

Painted in Olive Drab over Neutral Gray and wearing invasion stripes, "Berlin Express," P-51B-15-NA, serial number 43-24823, from the 363rd Fighter Squadron, 357th Fighter Group, flies a mission with a bubbletop Mustang. Formerly nicknamed "Old Crow" and flown by Capt. Clarence "Bud" Anderson of the 363rd Fighter Squadron, this plane was renamed "Berlin Express" when flown by Lt. William B. Overstreet. *Roger Freeman collection*

The pilot of P-51B-1-NA, serial number 43-12252, crashed into Lake Louisa, in Florida, on November 14, 1944. The aircraft was recovered from the lake in July 2001, and it was restored to flying condition. It was painted to replicate "Old Crow," P-51B-15-NA, serial number 43-24823, and fuselage code B6-S, from the 363rd Fighter Squadron, 357th Fighter Group, Eighth Air Force. It now bears civil registration number N551E. *Rich Kolasa*

Two 108-gallon drop tanks are mounted on the pylons under the wings of "Old Crow" as the P-51B buzzes an airfield. A noticeable departure from the preceding P-51A was the deeper cooling-air scoop on the belly. *Author*

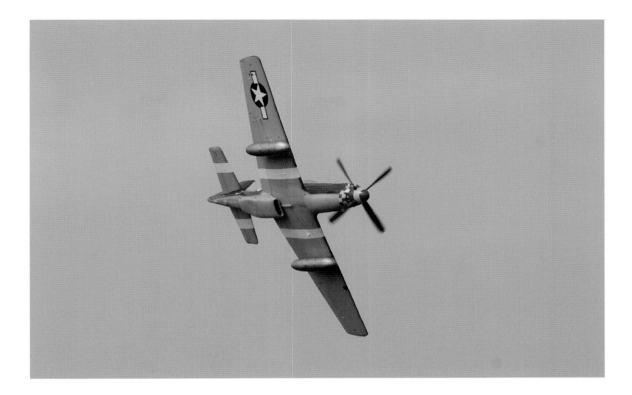

The carburetor air scoop on top of the cowling was omitted from the P-51A and replaced by a new air scoop below the propeller. This P-51B is equipped with the clear-bubble Malcolm hood, which was a British development used on the Mustang III to give the pilot a clearer and wider field of vision than that offered by the stock canopy. *Author*

As seen in a right-side view of the P-51B painted to match "Old Crow," the pitot tube was the L-shaped version and was mounted under the right wing. On the rear of the cooling-air scoop on the belly, the air exit flap is in the open position. This re-creation of "Old Crow" has a feature that the original plane lacked: a dorsal fin between the vertical stabilizer and the turtle deck. The change from the Allison V-1710 engine to the Merlin V-1650 in the P-51B caused stability problems in the aircraft; the dorsal fin was intended to improve stability and was a remedy that could be installed on planes in the field by using kits. *Rich Kolasa*

"Old Crow" has Hamilton Standard propellers with cuffs toward the bottoms of the blades. A small, bullet-shaped rear-view mirror is mounted above the windscreen. Two Browning .50-caliber machine guns were carried inside each wing; the firing ports in the right wing are visible above the bomb on the pylon. *Scott Taylor*

The red circle on the side of the fuselage, above the left bar of the national insignia, marks the fuel filler cap. The red, L-shaped marking on the flap was a reminder to crewmen not to step on the flap.
Rich Kolasa

The bulge engineered into the Malcolm hood is particularly visible from this angle. That bulge permitted the pilot better vision downward and to the rear than the stock canopy, with its flat side panels. In the foreground are the left horizontal stabilizer and the dorsal fin. *Scott Taylor*

The Malcolm hood on "Old Crow" apparently is a reproduction. The actual Malcolm hoods used on World War II Mustangs had only a bottom frame: instead of a metal front and rear frame, the Plexiglas was thicker in those areas, so that the clear hood formed its own front and rear frames. *Scott Taylor*

In a close-up of the right side of the cockpit, the track for the Malcolm hood of the restored P-51B correctly incorporates groups of rollers, in sets of three, with the exception of two rollers to the front. No reflector gunsight is installed above the instrument panel, but the stock ring-and-bead auxiliary sight is present: the ring is on the inside of the windscreen, and the bead is on a post to the front of the windscreen. Atop the windscreen is the rear-view mirror. *Scott Taylor*

The Malcolm hood on "Old Crow" is viewed close-up from the right side, also offering a good view of the curved section of canopy that is attached to the fuselage to the rear of the cockpit. Three small plates attached to the frame of the fixed canopy accommodate slotted screws, for removing the canopy panel in order to gain access to the radio equipment behind the pilot's headrest. *Scott Taylor*

CHAPTER 8
P-51C

The combination of the Mustang airframe with the Merlin power plant yielded a fighter that could hold its own against any of its contemporaries—plus, with the addition of drop tanks, it had the potential to provide long-range escort for the heavy bombing raids that were being conducted with increasing frequency.

Demand for those bombers, as well as warplanes in general, resulted in a serious shortage of labor in areas around aircraft-manufacturing centers, especially in California. North American began making plans to build a plant in Grand Prairie, near Dallas, Texas, where labor and electricity were plentiful. Concurrently, the federal government, through the Defense Plant Corporation, was also investigating building an aircraft plant in the Dallas area. The government, while concerned about the West Coast labor situation, also feared seaborne enemy air strikes. In the end, the government built the plant and leased it to North American to operate. During the course of the war, the Defense Plant Corporation built several aircraft plants inland, which in turn were to be operated by contractors.

At about the same time that plans were being made to open a Texas plant, a plant was opened in Kansas City. T-6 Texan production was shifted entirely to Dallas, and B-25 production to Kansas City, freeing the Inglewood facility to produce solely the Mustang. However, even that was not enough, and plans were made to build the Mustang in Grand Prairie as well.

Mustang production began in Grand Prairie—a town referred to as "Dallas" by North American and the Army—with aircraft that were near duplicates of the P-51B, which were designated P-51C.

The first P-51C took to the air on August 5, 1943, which was only three months to the day after the first flight of the P-51B. When P-51C production began, it utilized the Packard Merlin V-1650-3, the same as the P-51B at that time. This engine was rated at 1,400 horsepower at takeoff and 1,450 horsepower at 19,800 feet.

Beginning with the P-51C-5-NT and the P-51B-15-NA production blocks, the Merlin V-1650-7 engine was utilized instead. That engine developed 50 horsepower more at takeoff and had a war emergency rating of 1,695 horsepower.

Arguably even more significant than the increase in horsepower was a seemingly subtle change—the addition of an 85-gallon fuel tank behind the seat. Although when this tank was full, the directional stability of the Mustang was adversely affected, it did give the Mustang the range to reach Berlin and return to England. This of course meant that the Mustang could now escort the bombers for the duration of their missions to the German capital.

Because of the instability caused by the fuselage fuel tank, some units restricted the use of this tank to 65 gallons. In all cases, pilots would burn the fuel from the fuselage tank first, so as to recoup the Mustang's agility as quickly as possible.

While the addition of the fuselage fuel tank had a huge impact on the operational ability of the Mustang, externally it was almost imperceptible. More readily apparent was a change that happened during P-51B-10-NA and P-51C-1-NT production, at which time the Mustang lost its Olive Drab and Neutral Gray camouflage in favor of a natural-metal finish. As the Allied forces wrested control of the air, the need for camouflage was greatly diminished. Eliminating paint reduced the weight of the aircraft, lessened drag, and obviously lowered cost.

In October 1943, the first of the Merlin-powered Mustangs reached Europe in the hands of the US 354th Fighter Group. The Commonwealth, not surprisingly, also received the Merlin-powered Mustang, designating the type Mustang III. In fact, it was in the hands of the British that the next major innovation to the type was introduced. The framework of the originally designed canopy introduced numerous blind spots, which obviously was a real handicap for a fighter aircraft, where oftentimes the pilot who spots the enemy first wins.

In order to dispense with the framed canopy, North American engineers in England worked with the RAF to create a frameless blown Perspex canopy similar to that designed for the smaller Spitfire. Once the design was complete, the British firm R. Malcolm and Company began production of the modification kits. The kits were rather extensive, and 135 man-hours were required per aircraft for installation. Canopy side rails had to be installed on the fuselage, along with an internal structure to support those rails, and a hand-crank mechanism had to be installed. The front and rear edges of the hood were thick frosted Plexiglas, with the only metal in the hood itself being the side rails. The hood was designed this way so that should it have to be jettisoned in an emergency, it would shatter on the rudder, rather than become fouled in it.

Soon, almost all RAF Mustang IIIs were equipped with the hoods, as were many USAAF P-51B and P-51C aircraft, with a deliberate effort being made to fit the new canopy to all the aircraft.

As demand for the Mustang increased, not only did it outstrip the capacity of North American's Inglewood, California, plant, but huge demand for aircraft caused the labor pool in that area to be exceeded as well. Thus, in 1943, a second production line for the Mustang was set up in Grand Prairie, near Dallas, Texas. The first Mustangs produced in that facility were 1,750 P-51B duplicates designated as P-51Cs. USAAF serial number 43-25148 is an example of a P-51C-10-NT. The suffix NT in the aircraft designation signified that it was built at Grand Prairie, sometimes referred to as Dallas, rather than at Inglewood. *Stan Piet collection*

P-51Bs, or Cs, are under assembly at a North American Aviation plant. The wings and rudders of these planes have been sprayed with primer, but the fuselages are bare Alclad. On each of these Mustangs, the inlet for the carburetor air duct has been taped over to keep out foreign objects, and the doors for the machine gun bays are in the open position. *American Aviation Historical Society*

Several P-51Cs are included in this group of razorback Mustangs at a desert airbase. In the foreground is serial number 42-103804, while to the right is 42-103808; both are P-51C-1-NT Mustangs. All the aircraft have codes beginning with the letter *F* on the cowlings. *National Archives*

In the cockpit of this P-51C is Captain Andrew D. Turner, commanding officer of the 100th Fighter Squadron, 332nd Fighter Group, the famed "Tuskegee Airmen." Capt. Turner waves from the cockpit of his fighter at a 15th Air Force base in September 1944. *National Museum of the United States Air Force*

This P-51C-5-NT, USAAF serial number 42-103362, crashed upon landing at RAF Bottisham, England, on 30 May 1944, due to brake failure. The plane was assigned to the 374th Fighter Squadron, 361st Fighter Group, and Lt. Loy C. Vandiver was the pilot. *National Museum of the United States Air Force*

The British received some 944 P-51Bs and P-51Cs and designated the types together as Mustang III. This Mustang III exhibits an RAF serial number (FX883), camouflage scheme, and tricolor flash on the tail but has the US national insignia, indicating that this photo was in all likelihood taken in the United States, prior to delivery. *National Archives*

The natural-metal finish of P-51C-5-NT, serial number 42-103433, glistens in the sun as it rests in the dispersal area of an air base in England. This aircraft was one of just over 200 P-51C aircraft that were converted to F-6C reconnaissance birds. *Stan Piet collection*

Assigned to the 359th Fighter Group when this photo was taken, 42-103433 was reassigned to the 15th Tactical Reconnaissance Squadron, 10th Photo Reconnaissance Group. The aircraft was involved in a taxiing accident with another F-6C on April 15, 1945, with William L. Meikle at the controls, while based at Ober-Ulm, Germany. *Stan Piet collection*

"Mr. Hot Nuts III," a P-51C, has three German flag kill markings to the rear of the engine-access panels of the cowling. Between the Mustang and the massive hangar in the background is another North American Aviation aircraft, the AT-6 Texan advanced trainer. *National Museum of the United States Air Force*

North American P-51C-1-NT, serial number 42-103305 and fuselage code 6N-U, from the 505th Fighter Squadron, 339th Fighter Group, lies in a field after a takeoff accident at its home base, RAF Fowlmere, England, on May 12, 1944. This Mustang was written off two days later. A red-and-white checkerboard scheme was painted on the nose; the propeller spinner was white with a red band. *National Museum of the United States Air Force*

A line of P-51 Mustangs and a lone Lockheed P-38 Lightning in the background at RAF Debden include a two-seat trainer in the foreground, painted in a medium blue and with a Malcolm hood over the rear cockpit and the "VF" squadron code for the 336th Fighter Squadron, 4th Fighter Group. The other P-51s are bubbletops, coded as follows: CV-Q, from the 368th Fighter Squadron, 359th Fighter Group; LC-D, from the 77th Fighter Squadron, 20th Fighter Group; LH-V, of the 350th Fighter Squadron, 353rd Fighter group; and C5-Q, with the 364th Fighter Squadron, 357th Fighter Group. *Roger Freeman collection*

One of only a handful of surviving C-model Mustangs, P-51C-10-NT, serial number 42-103831, flew in several Bendix Races after World War II and was restored by Cal Pacific Airmotive, of Salinas, California, in the 1980s. It has been painted to replicate "Ina, the Macon Belle," the P-51C of Lt. Lee "Buddy" Archer, a highly decorated member of the 332nd Fighter Group, the "Tuskegee Airmen." Archer named the aircraft after his wife, Ina. *Rich Kolasa*

The Commemorative Air Force acquired P-51C-5-NT, serial number 42-103645, in the 1980s, and restored it to flying condition under the nickname "TUSKEGEE Airmen," civil registration number N61429. The plane was delivered on April 7, 1944, and served as a Stateside trainer in World War II. It was displayed at Montana State College (now Montana State University) for forty years. The CAF took possession of the aircraft in the late 1980s, and returned it to flying condition in 2001, giving it the "Red Tail" paintwork of the Tuskegee Airmen, the African-American pilots and personnel of the 322nd Fighter Group. *Scott Taylor*

In a close-up view of the forward part of "TUSKEGEE Airmen" from the left side, The red propeller spinner and the yellow and red stripes on the front of the cowling are displayed. Behind the open side panel of the canopy is the emblem of the CAF. Regrettably, Don Hinz, who spearheaded the foundation of the CAF's Red Tail Squadron, died of injuries while making an emergency landing in this plane at an air show in 2004. Subsequently, the aircraft was fully restored. *Scott Taylor*

The Service Group at RAF Debden, England, converted North American P-51B-1-NA, serial number 43-12193, to a TP-51B, a dual-control, two-seat trainer, for the 335th Fighter Squadron, 4th Fighter Group, in World War II. The "WW" before the tail number indicated "war weary." *Roger Freeman collection*

The tandem cockpits of TP-51B, serial number 43-12193, are observed from the left side with the top and side panels of the canopy open. Clearly, the rear cockpit was very cramped, since the rear seat was very close behind the front seat, and what appears to be a crash pad was mounted to the rear of the trainee's front seat, to protect the instructor's face in the event of a rough landing or crash.
Roger Freeman collection

Pilots from the 4th Fighter Group, 8th Air Force, pose next to a two-seat P-51 trainer aircraft at RAF Debden. This trainer has the Malcolm hood over the rear cockpit. Note that the spoked wheel on the main landing gear, the rear-view mirror on the windscreen, and the stripe on the cowling are painted the same shade of red as the nose.
Roger Freeman collection

An instructor has wriggled into the rear seat of a Mustang training aircraft assigned to the 4th Fighter Group at RAF Debden. The design of the red area on the nose is in the style used on P-51s of that fighter group. *Roger Freeman collection*

The Collings Foundation, in Stow, Massachusetts, acquired P-51C, serial number 42-103293, and then, in 2002–2003, converted it to a TP-51C dual-seat, dual-control trainer, nicknamed "Betty Jane." The plane was constructed at North American Aviation's Dallas plant. An extra section of canopy was added aft of the stock canopy, and a rear seat with full controls and instruments was installed. Red stripes, for extra visibility, as befits a trainer aircraft, were applied to the empennage. *Rich Kolasa*

The Collings Foundation's North American P-51C/TP-15C conversion is seen from the right rear, providing a clear view of the red stripes applied to the empennage. The "CM" code below the rear canopy represents the 78th Troop Carrier Squadron, 435th Troop Carrier Group. *Rich Kolasa*

Both cockpits of the Collings Foundation's P-51C converted to a TP-51C trainer aircraft are viewed from the left side. Minute details of the interiors of the fold-down side panels of the canopy are visible, including the release handle for the forward panel, with a yellow knob on the end. Modern instrument panels are present in the front and rear cockpits. *Rich Kolasa*

"Betty Jane," the TP-51C conversion, is viewed from the front right, with flaps lowered. Below the right wing, and in line with the outboard edge of the flap, is the pitot tube. *Rich Kolasa*